Tell Me Why

WHY?

The Moon Changes Shape

Kathryn Beaton

Published in the United States of America by Cherry Lake Publishing
Ann Arbor, Michigan
www.cherrylakepublishing.com

Content Adviser: Matthew Linke, Planetarium Director, State Chair, Great Lakes Planetarium
Association (GLPA), University of Michigan Museum of Natural History Planetarium
Reading Adviser: Marla Conn, ReadAbility, Inc.

Photo Credits: © Pete Pahham/Shutterstock Images, cover, 1, 7; © Dalton Dingelstad/Shutterstock
Images, cover, 1, 15; © Digital Media Pro/Shutterstock Images, cover, 1, 19; © G-ZStudio/
Shutterstock Images, cover; © Voraorn Ratanakorn/Shutterstock Images, cover; © Lori Mitchell/
Shutterstock Images, cover, 7; © Balazs Kovacs Images/Shutterstock Images, 6; © Weldon
Schloneger/Shutterstock Images, 9; © Designua/Shutterstock Images, 11; © MountainHardcore/
Shutterstock Images, 13; © Traveller Martin/Shutterstock Images, 15; © gilas/Thinkstock, 17;
© Carolina K. Smith MD/Shutterstock Images, 19; © bikeriderlondon/Shutterstock Images, 21

Library of Congress Cataloging-in-Publication Data

Beaton, Kathryn, author.
  The moon changes shape / Kathryn Beaton.
      pages cm. -- (Tell me why)
  Summary: "Young children are naturally curious about the world around
them. The Moon Changes Shape offers answers to their most compelling
questions about the lunar phases. Age-appropriate explanations and appealing
photos encourage readers to continue their quest for knowledge. Additional
text features and search tools, including a glossary and an index, help
students locate information and learn new words."—Provided by publisher.
  Audience: Ages 6-10.
  Audience: K to grade 3.
  Includes bibliographical references and index.
  ISBN 978-1-63362-000-1 (hardcover) -- ISBN 978-1-63362-039-1 (pbk.) --
ISBN 978-1-63362-078-0 (pdf) -- ISBN 978-1-63362-117-6 (ebook) 1.
Moon--Phases--Juvenile literature. 2. Moon--Juvenile literature. I. Title.

QB588.B38 2015
523.3'2--dc23
                              2014031827

Cherry Lake Publishing would like to acknowledge the work of The Partnership for
21st Century Skills. Please visit www.p21.org for more information.

Printed in the United States of America
Corporate Graphics

Table of Contents

Full Moon Over the Farm

Nick was excited! He had just arrived at his grandma's farm to spend the summer there. The first night, sitting with Grandma on the front porch, Nick saw a **full moon**.

"Look!" he said. "It's so bright tonight and it's a perfect circle."

"That's right," his grandma said. "But we don't see a full moon all the time."

Away from the bright lights of the city, you can see the moon more clearly.

Nick thought about that. "I know the moon is a **sphere**," he said, "just like the sun."

"You're right," she said. "But we don't always see it that way. Let's keep watching the moon together. And when you notice it changing, you can draw a little picture on my calendar."

That night, Nick drew the moon as a perfect circle. He wondered how long it would stay that way, and what would happen next.

MAKE A GUESS!

Does the moon look the same in the United States as it does in Australia? Visit your library or go online with an adult and find out.

The moon may look like a flat circle, but it's more like a ball.

7

Twenty-Nine Days

A week passed. Nick realized that the moon was the shape of a half-circle. "That's weird," he said. "What happened?"

"The moon itself is the same size it always is," Grandma said. "And the sun is still shining on half of it. What changes is how much of that sunlit part we can see."

She explained that the moon **orbits** Earth about every 29 days. Earth is also orbiting the sun. The lighted surface of the

Half of the moon is always lighted by the sun.

moon will appear bigger or smaller to us, depending on where the moon is in its orbit. We call these different views of the moon **lunar phases**. *Lunar* means "moon."

"How many lunar phases are there?" Nick asked.

"That's a tricky question," Grandma said. "Some people say four, or eight, or even more. Scientists don't always agree."

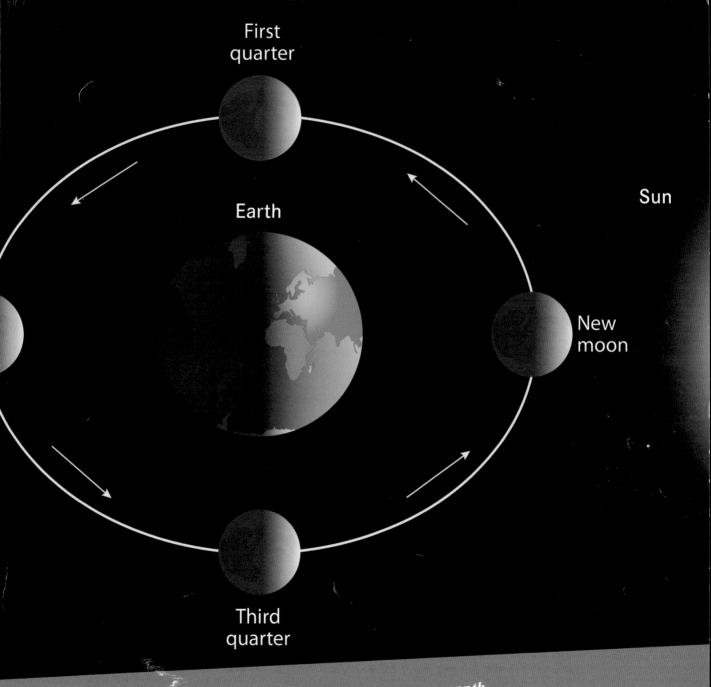

First
quarter

Earth

Sun

New
moon

Third
quarter

These are the phases of the moon that happen every month,
when the moon orbits the earth once.

The Moon Goes Missing

Soon, the moon began to rise very late at night. Nick went to sleep too early to see it, but then the moon was still there in the morning.

One day, a tiny sliver of the moon was visible all day long. Grandma explained that this meant a **new moon** was almost here. A new moon is when the moon moves between the earth and the sun. The half facing us is completely dark.

This crescent moon is almost a new moon.

"This is a normal part of the orbit?" Nick asked. "The moon is still up there, but without any sunlight on it?"

"The sun is still shining on the half that's not facing us," Grandma reminded him. "We can't see the moon tonight at all."

She had set up an easel and was mixing some oil paints.

"What are you painting?" Nick asked.

Grandma laughed. "It's a surprise. You can't see this tonight either."

ASK QUESTIONS!

Do other planets have moons that orbit them? Visit a library or go online with an adult to find the answer.

The moon is always orbiting Earth, even when we can't see it.

A few days later, Nick noticed that the moon was back at sunset. He saw a skinny, lighted edge of the moon very near the setting sun. Grandma said that this was called a crescent moon and pointed out that it was lighted on the right edge.

"Bright right, growing light!" she said. This came true over the next two weeks. Nick could see more and more of the moon each night. More of the lighted side of the moon was facing the earth.

The moon doesn't change shape, but we see it from a different viewpoint.

Back to the Beginning

Eventually, the moon looked full again. It was the same perfect circle Nick had seen the first night of his visit.

"Wow," Nick said. He drew in the last entry on his chart—a white circle. "The moon is back where it started."

But he could see that the real moon had shadowy splotches that he hadn't drawn in. "What are those big, gray spots?"

Do you see spots on the moon in this photograph? What do you see? A human face? A rabbit?

There are thousands of large craters, or holes, on the moon, and there could be millions of small craters.

"I've never gotten close enough to check," Grandma said, smiling. "But I read that they are huge lakes of hardened **lava**."

The next morning, Nick's dad came to pick him up. "See you later, my little **astronomer**," Grandma said. She handed him the painting she'd finished. It was Nick staring up at a full moon!

A telescope makes something far away seem larger and closer.

Think About It

Many cultures around the world have folktales about people living on the moon. Visit your library or go online with an adult to find out more about moon myths.

People have been studying the moon for hundreds of years, but scientists still have questions. What are some of your questions?

What phase was the moon in on the day or night you were born? Go online with an adult and look for a moon phase calendar.

Glossary

astronomer (uh-STRON-uh-mer) someone who studies outer space

full moon (FUHL MOON) the moon when its whole front face is lit up

lava (LAH-vuh) molten rock that comes from a volcano

lunar phases (LOO-ner FAY-ziz) the recurring patterns of sunlight on the moon

new moon (NOO MOON) when the moon comes between the earth and the sun, and is not visible

orbits (OR-bits) takes a curved path around another object

sphere (SFEER) a perfect circle, in solid ball-like form

Find Out More

Books:

Driscoll, Michael. *A Child's Introduction to the Night Sky: The Story of the Stars, Planets, and Constellations, and How You Can Find Them in the Sky*. New York: Black Dog and Leventhal Publishers, 2004.

Krautwurst, Terry. *Night Science for Kids: Exploring the World After Dark*. New York: Lark Books, 2005.

Wagner, Kathi, and Sheryl Racine. *The Everything Kids' Astronomy Book: Blast into outer space with stellar facts, intergalactic trivia, and out-of-this-world puzzles*. Fort Collins, CO: Adams Media, 2008.

Web Sites:

The Kid Should See This—Phases of the Moon
http://thekidshouldseethis.com/post/22623876256
This short video shows the moon cycling through its different phases.

The Old Farmer's Almanac for Kids—Moon Phase Calendar
www.almanac4kids.com/sky/thismonth.php
See what phase the moon was in on any day going back to 1902!

Index

About the Author

Kathryn Beaton lives and writes in Ann Arbor, Michigan.